Lobola

Its implications for women's reproductive rights

in Botswana, Lesotho, Malawi, Mozambique, Swaziland, Zambia and Zimbabwe

WL SA

Women and law

In Southern Africa Research Trust

WEAVER
W
—PRESS—

WEAVER

W

-PRESS-

Distributed by Weaver Press
P.O.Box 1922 Avondale Harare Zimbabwe

Published by Women and Law in Southern Africa Research Trust (WLSA)
Regional Office 2002
16 Lawson Avenue, Milton Park, Harare
P.O.Box UA71, Union Avenue, Harare, Zimbabwe
© WLSA, Regional Office

ISBN: 1-77915-006-7
Cover and title page photograph: John Akester
Other inside photographs: Biddy Partridge
Design and layout: Margo Bedingfield
Origination: Crystal Graphics

About the authors

Sarah C. Mvududu is a sociologist and the WLSA regional co-ordinator.

Chikadzi Joseph is a social scientist and the full-time research associate, Botswana.

Puleng Letuka is a lawyer and the full-time research associate, Lesotho.

Keiso Matashane-Marite is social scientist and the national co-ordinator, Lesotho.

Dorothy Kaunda is a lawyer and the full-time research associate, Malawi.

Eulalia Tembo is a social scientist and the national co-ordinator, Mozambique.

Zakhe E. Hlanze is a social scientist and the full-time research associate, Swaziland.

Priscilla Chileshe is a social scientist and the full-time research associate, Zambia.

Tsitsi Nzira is a nurse by profession and the full-time research associate, Zimababwe.

Special acknowledgement

WLSA is very grateful for the financial assistance from HIVOS in producing this book. Without them it would not have been possible.

Contents

List of cases

Mathibeli v Chabalala (CIV/APN/76/85)
Jena v Nyemba

List of Acts

Legal Age of Majority Act, 1982,
Customary Marriages Act Chapter 5:07
Matrimonial Causes Act, Chapter 5:13

1 Introduction

WLSA research has indicated that the power struggle between women and men within the institution of marriage revolves around issues of control over decision-making and marital resources which include sexuality, husband's and wife's incomes, marital property, children, succession and inheritance.

In addition, most of the WLSA countries operate a plural legal system of marriage that includes general law and customary law. Under both systems, the position of women within a marriage is not equal to that of men in terms of power and decision-making.

The practice of paying *lobola* is common in all the seven WLSA countries, although it is called by different names and usually precedes any marriage — civil, Christian or customary. This is despite the fact that under the general laws of these countries *lobola* is not a requirement for the solemnization of a civil marriage. This situation highlights a common feature of all systems of marriage in these countries — the patriarchal ideology where men dominate the marriage process and control the decision-making power through the practice of *lobola*.

The concept of *lobola* and its implications for women's rights in the seven WLSA countries, namely Botswana, Lesotho, Malawi, Mozambique, Swaziland, Zambia and Zimbabwe, is the subject of analysis for this monograph. *Lobola* is a practice that determines the formation of a marriage. The importance of its application in determining the existence and validity of marriage differs in the seven WLSA countries from one ethnic group to another and from family to family. This is because southern Africa is characterized by multi-ethnic, multi-cultural, multi-lineage and multi-racial socio-political and economic diversity.

The seven WLSA countries share a similar historical legacy of colonial administration that has had the effect of reducing plural social and legal systems into a dual system. This factor will be shown to have widened the application of *lobola* to ethnic groups which historically did not have this practice. In addition, these countries face the challenges of widening poverty, liberalization of economies and inherent globalization which in turn have affected the value systems by which family formations are measured. The historical symbolism of *lobola* as a token of appreciation on the part of the groom's family has shifted to take the form of a commercial transaction. For instance, the majority of ethnic groups in Zambia, Malawi and Mozambique are matrilineal and do not place any importance on *lobola* whereas the

The historical symbolism of lobola as a token of appreciation on the part of the groom's family has shifted to take the form of a commercial transaction.

universality of its application can be noted in countries such as Botswana, Lesotho, Swaziland and Zimbabwe. Even though this practice has universal application in these countries, the extent of determining the validity of marriage varies. In some countries it is a prerequisite for marriage while in other countries it is not necessarily a sole determinant of marriage.

The analysis focuses on the contextual background and the historical perspectives of how the practice of *lobola* evolved into its present form. It unfolds the dynamics of a practice that has been defined broadly by historians and social anthropologists (Schapera *et al.*, 1938, 1963) as a basis for cultural identification. Counter arguments are also presented within a human rights framework that locate women who are at the centre of this practice as objects of commodification and profit-making.

The different types of marriage regimes and their implications for women's rights in the seven southern African countries of WLSA are also examined, as well as the concept of marriage.

...lobola has to be understood within a context of plural legal systems...

Theoretical framework and critical concepts

The critical concepts identified for an in-depth understanding of *lobola* are marriage, custom, rights, personhood and productive and reproductive rights. These concepts will be discussed , taking into account the multi-faceted dimension of family law in the seven southern African countries. For instance, *lobola* has to be understood within a context of plural legal systems whereby some laws are sanctioned by the state, some by customs and others are the living laws that guide the practices of the majority of people in the region. The importance of plurality of laws and people's adherence to living law has been documented by WLSA research.

Before exploring the meanings of the critical concepts cited above, it is important to interrogate the meaning of the concept of *lobola* itself. Where was it derived from? What does it mean? What is its significance to the debate on women's reproductive, productive, sexual and other rights? The concept will be examined from a feminist perspective which allows us to show how the practice of *lobola* affects women. The feminist framework helps us to develop a critical understanding of the social relations within which the practice of *lobola* operates and the way it structures women's sexual and reproductive rights.

Lobola will be shown to have been an element in the social

organization of society which served the function of binding families together. So where it was practised, payment took the form of whatever was the dominant resource and main economic activity. Among the cattle-keeping people it took the form of cattle. *Lobola* will be shown to raise a number of issues that mostly emanate from its definition. The theoretical perspectives section raises the multi-dimensional issues surrounding *lobola* — why it is regarded as a women's rights issue.

The analysis questions the universal application of lobola in southern Africa and shows the extent to which it determines the validity and existence of marriage.

The analysis questions the universal application of *lobola* in southern Africa and shows the extent to which it determines the validity and existence of marriage. For instance, in Botswana, *bogadi* is just one part of a long process of acquiring a wife or *patlo*. *Bogadi* is in most cases the last part of numerous lengthy negotiations and is paid to transfer the rights of the children from their mother's family to their father's. However, the proponents of the practice view the original purpose of *bogadi* as a gesture of thanks from the man's family to the woman's family. Some see it as compensation to the wife's family for the loss of their daughter's services (Schapera, 1933/4: 144). In Lesotho, *bohali* is required to validate a customary marriage. In the case of Zimbabwe, *lobola* is perceived as a symbol of unity between the families of the bride and groom. However, it has been argued that because some brides' parents demand hefty *lobola* payments from sons-in-law, they conclude that they are paying the fathers-in-law back all the money they spent on educating their daughter (Chigwedere, 1982).

The issue of personhood will be shown to emerge as a concern because of the implied transaction of women through lobola.

The issue of personhood will be shown to emerge as a concern because of the implied transaction of women through *lobola*. The arguments advanced touch on issues of violations of women's rights to dignity, to self-worth and to the respect of bodily integrity as enshrined in various international conventions and agreements such as the Convention for the Elimination of all forms of Discrimination Against Women (CEDAW), the SADC Gender and Development Declaration of September 1997, the African Charter on Human and People's Rights and the International Covenant on Social, Economic and Cultural Rights which almost all the seven WLSA countries are party to.

The analysis begins with this introduction then proceeds to look at *lobola* in context in Section Two. Section Three examines the various marriage regimes in the seven countries and their implications for women and girls, while Section Four focuses on the rights of women. The last section puts forward some recommendations and outlines possible areas of action.

2 Lobola in context

This section explores the meaning of *lobola* by examining the historical context in which the practice of *lobola* took place in the seven southern African countries where WLSA operates, as well as the current practices and their social, economic and cultural consequences for women and girls.

The seven WLSA countries share a common historical background of colonization. Six of the countries were colonized by Britain, while Mozambique was colonized by Portugal. In all these countries a dual legal system is a common legacy, occasioned by the colonial policies that decided that customary law would apply to the indigenous people of a colonized territory while the received law would apply to the settlers.

This duality is also reflected in the economies of these countries as laws developed to deal with commercial interests as a matter of priority. Colonization had an impact on the practice of *lobola* as this analysis will show and so did the introduction of the money economy.

Lobola is a customary or cultural practice found in the seven WLSA countries and is part of the marriage process. *Lobola* has a long history, although it has no universal meaning or application. *Lobola* was practised almost exclusively in this southern African sub-region by patrilineal groups. It was not practised amongst most matrilineal groups.

Of the seven WLSA countries, Botswana, Lesotho, Swaziland and Zimbabwe are predominantly patrilineal societies where descent is traced through the father's line. The various ethnic groups found in these countries practise *lobola*. The remaining three countries of Mozambique, Malawi and Zambia are predominantly matrilineal societies where *lobola* was hardly practised. In Malawi and Mozambique none of the matrilineal groups had the practice.

Lobola in the southern African context historically reflected the communal nature of African life. It also reflected traditional values. For instance, in most societies an individual belonged to the extended family. Thus biological parents were not directly involved in the process of negotiating *lobola*, nor did they in certain situations benefit from it, rather it went to other members of the wider family. These people did not only receive the *lobola* but were obliged to assist the woman on whose behalf it had been received. In the event of divorce they were obliged to refund the bridegroom and his family where this was demanded in cases where the woman was considered at fault, for example,

> *Lobola in the southern African context historically reflected the communal nature of African life. It also reflected traditional values.*

due to barrenness or adultery. *Lobola* which historically was paid as cattle was, in turn, used to pay *lobola* on behalf of males in the family of the woman for whom the lobola was paid. Arnfred (1994) referring to the practice in southern Mozambique stated that:

> ...cattle received as *lobola* could be used for nothing else, that is the father receiving *lobola* for his daughter could not sell the cattle and build himself a bigger house. *Lobola* cattle was earmarked for *lobola* use.

Current *lobola* practices in the seven WLSA countries

Various terms are used to define *lobola* and there are a number of stages before a couple is considered married. In Botswana it is referred to as *bogadi* and in Lesotho it is *bohadi*. In Swaziland, Mozambique and among the Tumbukas of Malawi and the Ndebele of Zimbabwe, the practice is called *amalobolo*. Among the Shona-speaking people of Zimbabwe, the practice is referred to as *roora* while in Zambia it is called *malowolo* among the Ngonis, *impango* among the Bembas and *sionda* among the Lozi.

The term *lobola* is defined as the process where the family of the man makes payments to the family of the woman in the process of marriage. In all the seven WLSA countries, the practice of *lobola* was comprised essentially of two parts: the introductory ceremony consisting of small payments or an exchange of gifts that mark the beginning of the marriage process and the main ceremony where major payments are made. Usually the small payments have to be paid before the main ceremony.

...the practice of lobola was comprised essentially of two parts: the introductory ceremony consisting of small payments or an exchange of gifts that mark the beginning of the marriage process and the main ceremony where major payments are made.

Introductory ceremony

Among the different groups the marriage process consists of an introductory ceremony during which some small payments or gifts are made or given to the girl's family. These have different meanings and implications. These include *vuramuromo* for the Shona in Zimbabwe or *chinjuramulomo* for the Tumbuka of Malawi which refer to a small payment that allows the bridegroom's party to open negotiations. When this payment is made,

Amongst the Tumbuka of Malawi and the Ngoni of Zambia, there is a payment for betrothal which binds someone with a promise to marry.

The significance of all these initial exchanges is that the prospective husband declares interest in the future wife.

then there is provision for the bride-to-be to take some money offered in a plate to signify her acceptance of the man seeking her hand in marriage. It is important to note that this is the only time the bride has a voice in the transaction.

Amongst the Tumbuka of Malawi and the Ngoni of Zambia, there is a payment for betrothal which binds someone with a promise to marry. This payment precedes the *malobolo* payments. For the Tumbuka, this payment is called *vikhole* and it is usually in the form of money or material gifts such as beads. This payment is given to the paternal aunts (*ankhazi*) of the bride-to-be who are the first people to whom the marriage proposal is made. The *vikhole* payment is determined by and, once paid, is only shared among all the bride's paternal aunts after they have purchased gifts for the bride to use during marriage. It is an outright gift that is not refundable. In terms of legal effects, betrothal does not confer on the parties the right of cohabitation and should they have sexual intercourse, the bride's father may seek compensation, termed *chibadala*. However, the man who is betrothed to the girl is also entitled to recover compensation from a third party that may make the girl pregnant.

In Lesotho, the process starts with the bridegroom's parents asking for the woman's hand in marriage from her parents. According to Maqutu (1992) the next step is to reach agreement on *bohali* cattle. In Zambia, the Tonga start with *muyumusho*, which refers to the eventual process of the bridegroom's family taking the bride away, while among the Ngoni it is *mfuko*. This could be in the form of an animal or tobacco. The significance of all these initial exchanges is that the prospective husband declares interest in the future wife.

In Swaziland, the marriage is said to have taken place once the female members of the groom's family have smeared the bride's face with red ochre (*libovu*). The matter of when the *lobola* is paid then rests with the groom's family who may take a very long time before they start paying.

On the other hand in Mozambique and among the Tsonga, the initial step is for the bridegroom's emissary to ask for water representing the nurturing role that the woman is expected to play. This is similar to the practice in Botswana where the bridegroom's party asks for *sego sa metsi* which is a water gourd. Among the Tswana of Botswana, once the bridegroom is given *sego sa metsi*, the process of *patlo* is entered into. This is the process of 'searching' for the girl that culminates in agreement

between the two families and what constitutes marriage. Dow and Kidd (1994) in their study on marriage and inheritance in Botswana quote a key informant, a headman, who said, '*Bohadi* is not marriage, agreement between parents is,' a statement that was also confirmed by other respondents in the same study. *Bohadi* gives the man rights over the children.

It is noteworthy that *patlo* involves giving gifts from the bridegroom's family to the bride's family. In most cases these include clothes for the bride, *ditukwe le ditsale* (head scarves and shawls) for the bride, her mother and aunts, *dijase* (coats) and *dihushe* (hats) for the bride's father and uncles and either a cow, goat or sheep or all of these. It is only after the *dilwana tsa patlo* have been given to the wife's family that they can be given the bride, even before the *bohadi* is paid.

There are a variety of other payments that are made before the main payments but the above are the significant payments that constitute the introductory ceremony.

...patlo involves giving gifts from the bridegroom's family to the bride's family.

The main ceremony

There are both similarities and differences in the composition of the main *lobola* ceremony in the seven WLSA countries. Similarities are payments for the bride's mother, her father and for the transfer of a woman's reproductive capacity from her natal family to the man's family. The differences are in what validates a marriage

For the Swazis the main ceremony, according to Maqutu (1992), comprises three cattle:

- *Khomo ea Seboko* is the cow which transfers the procreative function of the woman who is being married to the husband's family, clan and tribe.
- *Khomo ea thari Kapa letsoele* is the cow that is given to the mother in recognition of her role as the person who breastfed and nurtured the woman to marriageable age.
- *Khomo ea Thebe* is the cow given to the father to protect the woman in case the marriage fails.

In addition, other cattle are given to establish cordial relations, referred to as *lokhomo tsa sekhosi* in some instances, especially if the girl was a virgin. This was also practised among the Ngonis of Zambia. The parents of the boy could stop the marriage process if they thought the girl was not a virgin. However, this is a practice which has largely died out.

...The parents of the boy could stop the marriage process if they thought the girl was not a virgin.

In Swaziland, the main *lobola* consists of a minimum of twelve cattle, ten being the father's cattle and referred to as *emabheka*. The other two are the *insuulamnyembeti* beast (one that wipes away tears and is the mother's gift to acknowledge her nurturing role) and the *lugege* beast which is slaughtered on the day the main payment is delivered and marks the end of the marriage process. The beast is shared between the two families. More cattle are charged depending on how close a relative the girl is to the king (Hlapo, 1992). Although this is considered the main payment, it does not validate a marriage, it is only paid for a woman who has already been smeared with red ochre.

The main *lobola* exchange among the agro-pastoral Tsonga of Mozambique is cattle. However, the process is marked by negotiations until the two families agree on the number of cattle to be paid. Other items which are part of this process include clothes given to the father and mother of the bride, five metres of local *citenge* material for the bride's mother, a walking stick for the maternal grandmother and *mfuko wafole* which is tobacco used to communicate with ancestral spirits. It is only after all these requirements are met that a marriage is considered contracted.

The Ndebele and Shona of Zimbabwe have similar requirements for the main payment called respectively *sibaya* and *danga* (father's cattle). Among the Ndebele this consists of ten head of cattle which are only transferred or paid after two or three children are born. Among the Shona the main payment consists of anything from four to ten cattle and it is possible to pay cash at a negotiated price of Z$10 000–Z$15 000[1] per beast. This is similar to *malowolo* of the Ngonis of Zambia which consists of anything from one to twelve cattle. This signifies that *lobola* is paid for the woman's reproductive capacity and it is usually considered the woman's fault if there are no children born in the marriage. Thus where the *lobola* has been paid and there are no children born of that marriage, traditionally the family of the woman is obliged to find a replacement for the bride or refund the *lobola*. This is the rationale behind the delayed payment.

Included in the *sibaya* is one animal for the mother referred to as *inkomo yohlanga*. For the Shona, the mother's cow

...where the lobola has been paid and there are no children born of that marriage, traditionally the family of the woman is obliged to find a replacement for the bride or refund the lobola.

[1] US$180–270 (official exchange rate) This can only be judged in the context of local incomes; it is a very large sum of money for any family to raise.

(*mombe yeumai*) is paid for separately as part of the main payment. Under both the Shona and Ndebele customary law systems, clothes for the bride's parents constitute an important part of the *lobola*.

Among the Tumbuka of Malawi, *chuma* is the final and main payment. The amount paid is determined by what the men of the family consider reasonable. The amount, once received, is supposed to be shared with maternal uncles of the bride-to-be. It is the *chuma* that is refundable should the wife's 'bad' behaviour lead to divorce. This is similar to the practice among the Tonga of Zambia where the payment called *ciko* is refundable on dissolution of the marriage. Under the Tonga customary practice, payment of *loloba* (*ciko*) is the responsibility of the matrikin and the patrikin which signifies that the marriage is not just for the parties getting married but the wider family.

The legal, social, economic and cultural consequences

From the foregoing, we can perhaps contend that the term *lobola* is a misnomer because among many groups that practise it, the term refers to a series of payments, each having its own significance. However there is a major payment that among certain groups constitutes *lobola*. Thus for as long as that part is not paid, the man is considered not married with the exception of Botswana and Swaziland. This is despite having exchanged the small gifts or the smaller payments having been made. In other contexts *lobola* refers to all payments made in the process of negotiating a marriage. However, *lobola* means different things in different contexts. In countries characterized by patrikin, it signifies the transfer of the woman's reproductive and productive rights to the man's group, thus locating the children born in a marriage in the father's family. If *lobola* has not been paid then such children belong to the maternal grandfather. In matrikin societies, it simply creates a basis for reciprocal duties and obligations between two families as the children belong to the mother's family.

Patrilineal societies generally tended to be cattle-keeping peoples and lobola was a means of moving cattle from one family to another.

Lobola was also related to production in the traditional economy which created relations for the exchange of other goods and services. Patrilineal societies generally tended to be cattle-keeping peoples and *lobola* was a means of moving cattle from one family to another. This movement of cattle created a complex network of rights and obligations that persisted over generations. The *lobola* gave presumptive rights over the woman's productive and reproductive capacities to the man's group. This is why death did not signify the end of a marriage.

Among the Tsonga of Mozambique, the Basotho of Lesotho, the Ngoni of Zambia, the Shona and Ndebele of Zimbabwe and the Tumbuka of Malawi, payment of *lobola* transferred the procreative function of the girl who was getting married to the family of her husband. The children she bore from that point would belong to the husband. On the other hand, among the matrilineal groups like the Bemba of Zambia payments for marriage did not transfer a woman's fertility to her husband's group. In fact, historically the man's service to his wife's family was what was important. The service marked the beginning of a long relationship between two groups based on reciprocity.

Lobola was a means of establishing relationships between groups of people and, once established, created a network of rights and obligations between the groups of people concerned. The woman on whose behalf the *lobola* was paid was bound to stay in that relationship because any decision of hers to move from such a relationship disturbed a whole network of obligations and duties. The value placed on marriage, especially for women, ensured that a woman remained in marriage in patrilineal societies. Marriages among matrilineal groups where no *lobola* was paid were viewed as unstable, particularly among groups that practised a matrilocal form of residence.

The value placed on marriage, especially for women, ensured that a woman remained in marriage in patrilineal societies.

At times the type of girl the man was marrying became an issue. While virginity was not so highly valued among some groups and was therefore not an issue, among the patrilineal groups such as the Swazi of Swaziland, the Ngoni of Zambia and Shona of Zimbabwe, for instance, a girl's virginity was a commodity treasured and guarded by her father which he passed on to her husband at marriage. This is why claims for damages in the courts were awarded to the father of the girl in recognition of the fact that, if not a virgin at marriage, she would be given away as 'damaged' and would not attract much *lobola*. It is clear that the woman was not in control of her body. It was owned and controlled by her father, then by her husband.

In all the seven southern African countries constituting WLSA, there is more than one marriage regime and all of them have the civil and customary law marriages. In all of these countries except Mozambique, the different types of marriages are recognized by the state as legal marriages. However, in Zimbabwe the customary marriage is fully recognized as long as it is registered; if not registered it is only recognized for purposes of spousal maintenance, status and rights of and over children of such a marriage.

For civil marriages in all the WLSA countries, the major requirement is the consent of the parties who are of majority age and if under age they must be assisted by their parents or guardians. If the parents or guardians unreasonably withhold their consent, the courts might grant it on application from the minor. The marriages are solemnized by a state-appointed marriage officer. The solemnization can be done at an approved government institution or at a church.

However, in some countries such as Zimbabwe, despite the fact that parental consent is no longer required and, by implication, *lobola* is no longer an essential ingredient for the validation of marriage following the Legal Age of Majority Act, 1982, very few African women would dare to marry or to register their marriages without the family being fully involved (Gwaunza, 1996). Under custom *lobola* is still required. If a woman's family discovers her marriage has taken place without their involvement they might alienate her from the family or deny her moral and other support if problems arose in the marriage. The groom's family would also culturally not view the woman as a wife.

If a woman's family discovers her marriage has taken place without their involvement they might alienate her from the family or deny her moral and other support if problems arose in the marriage.

It would appear that custom, social and family pressure and fear of alienation can interfere with a woman's choice to exercise the rights that the law gives her. For customary marriages, the constitution of the marriage is a long drawn-out process comprising of agreement between the parties — the man and the woman — except for Malawi and Swaziland where arranged marriages are still practised. Such arrangements may be made irrespective of whether the woman is young or relatively mature.

Lobola payments are made in stages and these confer specific rights to the man and his family. For example in Botswana, Zimbabwe, Zambia and Malawi the payment of small gifts by the man or his family confers on him the status of son-in-law but with limited rights. While they can live as husband and wife, he has no rights over the children until the main portion of *lobola* has been paid. However, among the matrilineal Tonga of Zambia payment of *lobola* does not give a man rights over children. These are part of the mother's matrikin and their rights to inheritance are through their mother's brothers.

For Lesotho and Mozambique, after the parties have agreed

on the *lobola*, the groom's family will bring a portion of it and if this is acceptable to the bride's parents, then the man and woman can live as husband and wife. However, for Lesotho the number of cattle paid must be more than six and this would give the man rights over the children as well. In the case of Mozambique, a non-specified down payment is made to the bride's parents and the full amount becomes due when her procreative capacity has been proved.

For Swaziland and Botswana, *lobola* is not a requirement for the validity of a marriage. The marriage comes about as soon as female members of the man's family have smeared red ochre (*libovu*) on the bride or agreements on the *patlo* have been met respectively. *Lobola*, however, has to be negotiated and a mode of payment agreed upon. But, like the other countries, it is only after the man has paid *lobola* that he assumes rights over the children.

As we interrogate the implications of various systems of *lobola* as found in the seven WLSA countries, you might agree with Halim (1994: 26) that:

> Women are stripped of the right to participate in the public sphere because of the sense of ownership that prevails in the relationship between women and men. This is visible in marriage. The woman is the subject matter of the contract of marriage rather than a party to it. These intimate relations are where the subordination of women begins and where dependency is institutionalized. Although women are forced into dependency that lasts for a lifetime, there are no safeguards for continued support of the woman by her husband in the case of divorce.

The husband is considered the head of the family and holds the decision-making power in all family matters.

The multiplicity of marriage regimes in the seven WLSA countries seems to suggest the existence of multiple problems for women because of their gender. The deciding factor is the social reality that men are the decision-makers in terms of whether the couple should marry and the type of marriage regime they can enter into.

In all of the marriages cited above women do not enjoy the same rights as their men. The husband is considered the head of the family and holds the decision-making power in all family matters. It would seem that marriages under all the regimes

undermine the socio-economic position of women.

Another factor that might account for the disadvantaged position of women is the fact that there is no lower age limit in customary marriages, the guiding principle being the physical maturity of the girl. For instance, in Swaziland and as happens in other countries, young girls are usually married off to older men. From the outset such relationships involve significant power imbalances from which it is extremely difficult and rare for a girl to carve out her own autonomy. This places the woman in a position of subservience with rights no less than those of labourers.

The process of negotiating marriage is between men. The bride, beyond acknowledging that she knows the man, has no say in the amount of *lobola* claimed. There have been instances where the parents have threatened to abandon the whole process if she interferes. The powerlessness of women is not only apparent in the bride but it also extends to her mother. This is illustrated by how the *lobola* is distributed between the two parents. In most of the WLSA countries the mother gets only one cow for having nurtured the bride while the father gets the rest of the *lobola*.

The changing values and levels of *lobola* from being symbolic to a stage where it is almost a commercial venture has further compromised the position of women. For example, parents peg the *lobola* at a certain level depending on such factors as:
- the girl's educational attainment;
- whether she has a job;
- whether she is a virgin.

This implies that the woman is being treated as a property for which a good price is negotiated.

If the husband's family feels that the *lobola* payment was too high, then they may take out their frustrations on her. Considering the harsh economic hardships that all the countries are experiencing, it may lead to her being violated as argued by Mpofu (1981):

> ...it stands to reason that a man who has paid dearly for his wife will expect very high returns from her. This clearly gives him the right and power to be the judge of his wife's performance and productivity as well as reproductive capacity.

The process of negotiating marriage is between men. The bride, beyond acknowledging that she knows the man, has no say in the amount of lobola claimed.

It has been suggested that the number of cattle charged as part of the main portion of lobola is proportionate to the number of children the woman is expected to produce.

Lobola also compromises the women's position because through it they are treated like commodities for which the purchase price can be reduced when they are regarded as imperfect. This is borne out by the fact that *lobola* can be reduced because the woman had a child before this marriage. This aspect of *lobola* is demeaning and insults women's dignity.

It has been suggested that the number of cattle charged as part of the main portion of *lobola* is proportionate to the number of children the woman is expected to produce. For instance in Zimbabwe and under Ndebele practice the usual charge is ten head of cattle for ten children. In Mozambique the expectation is that a woman is 'supposed to bring out all the children in her belly until God decides that it is enough'.

At the end of a successful marriage negotiation and once a woman has moved in with her marital family, she might consider that she is now one of them. However, she is still considered a stranger in this family and will not be fully incorporated until she has proved herself to be a good wife, daughter-in-law and mother. At the same time even her natal family no longer considers her as a full member. This places the woman in a vulnerable position whereby she does not assume full rights and protection from either family.

One of the premises under which customary law marriage was constituted was that it was an agreement between two families. This was believed to have a stabilising effect on marriages as neither of the spouses could unilaterally end the marriage. However, with the current reality of money being raised exclusively by the groom, this stabilising factor has been eroded. Looking at this from another perspective, the woman has perhaps been relieved of the burden of having to provide her productive capacity to the groom's wider family. On the part of the bride's family, however, individualizing *lobola* means that her father or guardian can claim the *lobola* for his personal gain. Should the bride experience problems that require part of the *lobola*, however, her options would be limited as it is only her father who would have used it to the exclusion of other family members.

From the foregoing, we can safely conclude that *lobola* ties or almost enslaves a woman to the man and his family. This is illustrated by the fact that many women who are victims of violence at the hands of their husbands seldom present the problem to their natal family since the family would already have 'eaten'

the *lobola*. In such a case the woman's only choice is to bear the violence. *Lobola* in this manner legitimizes violence against women in a marriage set-up. Even in cases where the *lobola* has not been given for the woman, if she goes to her natal family and presents her problem of being ill-treated by her husband, the family might offer no protection. On the contrary they might demand the rest of the *lobola*. This lack of protection may even result in the woman being killed, leaving her family still demanding the *lobola* over her corpse,[2] as has been reported in the Zimbabwe press.

Lobola makes the dissolution of a marriage difficult for women while men can simply abandon the first wife and find another one. The fact that divorce is tied to return of *lobola* might result in the couple simply separating informally. In Zimbabwe there is no legal action available for the dissolution of unregistered customary marriages. The limbo can go on for indefinite periods with negative implications for women. For example in Lesotho in the case of *Mathibeli v Chabalala* (CIV/APN/76/85, cited in Maqutu 1992: 105) a woman had been separated from her husband for more than twenty years. When she died the former husband successfully claimed the right to bury her even though at the time she was living with and had children with another man. This seems to negate the general assertion that *lobola* preserves marriages. It seems to permanently tie a woman to the man against her will without improving their relationship. So the marriage continues to exist in theory. The existence of a marriage in theory seems to give perpetual rights to the man who may continue to harass the woman a long time after they are separated, including forcing her to have sex with him or beating her for having relations with other men.

In addition, divorce in customary marriages has negative consequences for the woman in terms of property. Since marriage transfers the woman's productive power to her husband, what she earns is regarded by law as belonging to her husband. This was aptly put by Gubbay JA in the Zimbabwean case of *Jena v Nyemba* (cited in Ncube *et al.*, 1997: 29) who said:

> ...property acquired during a marriage becomes the husband's property whether acquired by him or his wife.

The fact that divorce is tied to return of lobola might result in the couple simply separating informally.

Since marriage transfers the woman's productive power to her husband, what she earns is regarded by law as belonging to her husband.

---

[2] This is a practice whereby the family of the deceased woman refuse to authorize and participate in the burial of their daughter until *lobola* is paid posthumously.

In Zimbabwe there are legal provisions (Customary Marriages Act Chapter 5:07) and where there is an unregistered customary marriage, the woman is entitled to *mawoko* (property acquired by a woman through her own industry) and *mombe yeumai* in Shona or *inkomo zohlanga* in Ndebele (the cow given to a woman as part of the *roora*). In the event of divorce from a registered customary marriage, she is entitled to a share of the property in terms of the Matrimonial Causes Act, Chapter 5:13; and in an unregistered customary marriage she can still claim a part of the property on the basis of a universal partnership. Some women, especially those in unregistered customary marriages, are still denied property rights despite these progressive developments.

In practice, however, even where the wife is the main breadwinner, as is increasingly the case in most of the countries, on divorce she will leave the marriage empty-handed. As a result of the economic structural adjustment programme (ESAP) and other economic changes, retrenchment of men is forcing women to seek employment or engage in informal trading. The system of marriage which regards property acquired during marriage as the husband's erodes the woman's capacity to acquire her own property. Is this not tantamount to economic discrimination and disempowerment?

In view of this disempowerment, how can she be in a position to negotiate about anything, including sexuality and safe sex (especially in view of the real threat of sexually transmitted diseases, including HIV/AIDS), whether to have children or not, the number or spacing of such children, and her general reproductive health requirements?

While custody matters are generally decided on the principle of the best interests of the child, guardianship of the children of the marriage is exclusively vested in the husband in civil rites marriages and in customary marriages of patrilineal societies.

The other important implication of *lobola* and marriage for women is the issue of child custody and guardianship. While custody matters are generally decided on the principle of the best interests of the child, guardianship of the children of the marriage is exclusively vested in the husband in civil marriages and in customary marriages of patrilineal societies. In the latter the deciding factor is whether *lobola* has been transferred or not. Under such circumstances the woman is excluded from being part of the product of her own body and labour. The effect of this practice is that sometimes women are forced to remain in abusive marriages in order to protect their interests in their children.

Failure to procreate can mean the end of a marriage for a woman. She might be returned to her natal family and the *lobo-*

la that was given for her demanded back. Alternatively another woman in her family such as a sister or brother's daughter might be designated substitute to her in the reproductive function. In such a case no additional *lobola* is payable even though the husband's family will be gaining additional labour. Thus *lobola* has the potential of even affecting the other females in her natal family. The polygynous situation so created might result in co-wife rivalry between siblings or aunt and niece.

One of the assumed functions of the family — natal or marital — is the 'protection' of the woman. This protection can in fact undermine her capacity to make decisions and therefore affect her status as a person. This means that if she is to assert her rights, especially in the public sphere such as the courts of law, she has to be represented by whoever is supposed to protect her. If she is still unmarried this has to be her father or another male representative and if married it will be her husband or her husband's heir or male relative. This was one of the major findings in the research into the justice delivery system by all WLSA countries.[3] In a way this means that by excluding women from the realm of the law, they can only exercise certain rights through men. Since the procreative role is exclusive to women, the foregoing implies that this right will not be exercisable through the courts of law. This may be one area that needs to be examined further and improved upon for women to be able to assert their rights fully in the public arena.

From the foregoing it appears that the amount of *lobola* charged, whether too much or too little, all seems to give control of the woman to the man or his family. This is compounded by the woman not owning her productive or reproductive capacity. Whatever the justification or purpose of *lobola*, it seems to be of little or no benefit to women. The only effect it seems to achieve

> *If a woman is to assert her rights, especially in the public sphere such as the courts of law, she has to be represented by whoever is supposed to protect her.*

[3] *In search of justice: Where do women go?*, WLSA Lesotho (2000).
In the shadow of the law: Women and justice delivery in Zimbabwe, WLSA Zimbabwe (2000).
The justice delivery system and the illusion of transparency, WLSA Mozambique (2000).
Charting the maze: Women in pursuit of justice in Swaziland, WLSA Swaziland (2000).
Chasing the mirage: Women and the administration of justice in Botswana, WLSA Botswana (2000).
In search of justice delivery: Women and the administration of justice in Malawi, WLSA Malawi (2000).
Women and justice: Myth or reality in Zambia, WLSA Zambia (2000).

is the perpetuation of the dependency of women on men while failing to recognize and appreciate the valuable contribution of women both to production and reproduction.

The analysis so far has focused mostly on issues where the validity of marriage depends on whether *lobola* has been paid or not. While *lobola* does contribute a lot to the problems that women experience in terms of their capacity to regulate their own lives, a question that then arises is whether the situation of women is any better in systems where *lobola* is not a requirement. It is acknowledged that in almost all societies of the world expectations from women are higher. However, it has also been strongly contended that *lobola* retards the woman's negotiating power and undermines the quest for equality of status between men and women.

... a question that ...arises is whether the situation of women is any better in systems where lobola is not a requirement.

As May (1987: 41) notes:

> The custom of *lobola* has lost much of its traditional and spiritual significance and has become highly commercialized, but it is the buttress of the whole present system of marriage and pervades every area of personal law.

Out of this charge, it is clear that women come out the major losers and as May (ibid) further contends:

> One thing is certain: as long as the *lobola* system exists (as it is), women will never be free and equal members of society because men will not regard them as such.

For those who view *lobola* as a uniquely African practice that should be treasured and preserved at whatever cost, there is a counter argument that the practice existed in many parts of the world but has been abolished because it presented many complications in the same way as experienced by women in our context.

Even within our context *lobola* is not always an issue, for example with regard to rights over children. This point is aptly illustrated by practices among the matrilineal societies of Zambia, Malawi, Mozambique and some parts of Zimbabwe.

The need to change becomes more critical under the ongoing regional and international debates calling for states to

accord women their rights. The operationalization of these debates have culminated in the various international and regional conventions, treaties and charters calling on member states to implement these accordingly. However, the lives of many women in the respective WLSA countries have not yet benefited from these instruments. If practices such as *lobola* and its negative implications for women change, then such efforts would have made a difference.

From the foregoing, it is clear that *lobola* means different things within the seven WLSA countries. In some cases it signifies marriage, in others it locates the children born in a relationship in the family of the man. Among the Tonga of Zambia, men have suggested that *lobola* payments are a deposit for inheritance of children born of that union. *Lobola* is now being practised by many ethnic groups that did not hitherto. This has contributed to its spread but within a changed context, with a decline in the influence of the extended family and the individual man paying the *lobola* on his own.

It is also apparent that it is a practice that serves to reinforce the subordinate position of women. The woman appears to be a commodity over whom negotiations are entered into with very little or no regard for what she feels. It also appears that *lobola* can effectively be used to stop a man and woman who love each other from marrying if the two families do not approve of the relationship. It is also open to abuse by those who stand to benefit from receiving *lobola* where young girls may be forced into early marriages and marriages to older men. This leads to a number of problems such as compromising the young girls' education and health, considering that the highest rate of seroprevalence in Africa is in the 19 to 24 year age group and is different for boys. Being married off to older men makes these young girls prospective widows at a young age, thus perpetuating a cycle of poverty.

It also appears that lobola can effectively be used to stop a man and woman who love each other from marrying if the two families do not approve of the relationship.

Lobola payments have always reflected the relations of production at a given point in the life of a given people. Thus for cattle-keeping pastoral groups, it was always cattle that was paid as *lobola*. In other societies, it was the service a person rendered that was important. In our context today, it is usually in the form of money. This is true even among pastoral people as a lot of cattle have been lost to overcrowding, drought and cattle disease.

In addition, *lobola* has lost its original meaning which placed a high value on women but now seems to overvalue her

Lobola payments have changed over time starting as small objects and small amounts of money and progressing to large and sometimes exorbitant figures.

reproductive role at the expense of her integrity and her health. *Lobola* payments have changed over time starting as small objects and small amounts of money and progressing to large and sometimes exorbitant figures. For example in Mozambique, Zimbabwe and Zambia *lobola* consisted of such objects as straw, metal rings and hoes, while in Swaziland it used to be a basin of sorghum. In Lesotho *lobola* used to consist of three cattle. However, as noted by Maqutu (1992), this has since changed from ten to fifteen in 1973 and to twenty head of cattle in 2001. In Zimbabwe, *lobola* charges among the Karanga of Masvingo range from Z$100 000 to Z$200 000.[4] Some of the factors leading to changes in the practice of *lobola* have been the introduction of a money economy, colonisation and Christianity. The introduction of a money economy has led to a change in social values where money and what it can buy has assumed more importance than human relations with women's role of childbearing being overvalued. Other changes have seen the transformation of the *lobola* transaction from being a family to an individual affair. This means that prospective husbands of today are no longer dependent on their families for *lobola* payments.

Those who are in employment and can afford it are free to marry whom they want without much parental or extended family influence.

Those who are in employment and can afford it are free to marry whom they want without much parental or extended family influence. What it means is that *lobola* payments are now negotiated between the prospective husband and the bride's father. This makes the practice more like any other commercial transaction and the woman more like the personal property of the man.

The duality of laws in the countries under analysis is another complicating factor. In Zimbabwe, although the Legal Age of Majority Act (1982) stipulates that at the age of 18 a person becomes a major and can marry without parental consent, thereby making *lobola* no longer a requirement for marriage, the practice still goes on for fear of social sanctions.

It is also clear that *lobola* creates ties that bind women even in dangerous relationships. What happens to a woman who wants to leave an abusive relationship, but cannot find money to refund the *lobola* that was paid? Most likely she will stay in that bad relationship. During studies into the laws of inheritance and the family in six WLSA countries, women said they were tied by

[4] US$ 1818–3700 (official exchange rate) Once again this is a very large sum of sum for an ordinary family to raise.

cattle in bad relationships as they were seen as means to access *lobola* as a resource. It is also *lobola* that ties women permanently to her husband's family even after his death and being forced to 'marry' one of them. If the woman refuses to be 'inherited' by any of his relatives (brother or nephew) she risks being chased away from the marital home leaving her children. If she is allowed to stay despite refusing to be 'inherited' she has to avoid having sexual relations with other men as this will meet with severe sanctions as revealed by one widow in the WLSA Zimbabwe study into women and crime. The widow ended up in prison for criminal abortion which she committed when she found herself pregnant a few years after the death of her husband. She said she feared that if the husband's relatives found out that she was pregnant, she risked being forced to leave the marital home without her children, (WLSA, Zimbabwe, 2001). This again indicates that the sexual and reproductive rights of a woman are owned not just by her husband, but by members of his family as well, even after the death of the husband.

Lobola also affects a woman's capacity to decide on the number of children she can have in a marriage. She is viewed as a child-bearing machine and sometimes cannot decide on the number of children to bear. This may compromise the woman's ability to negotiate for safe sex , thus further predisposing her to the deadly HIV virus. We can therefore argue that *lobola* payments put women at high risk of the infection.

Women's sexual and reproductive rights do need rethinking on the question of *lobola* because they comprise their rights in marriage. *Lobola* has changed a lot as the context in which it is practised continually changes. The value system that underpinned the practice has also changed. In the process of change it has become open to abuse. Abuse has crept in through commercialization of the transaction and through greed. This has led to a situation where in its present form it can be interpreted as an abuse of women's and girls' rights. Hence there is a need to revisit the *lobola* concept, its practice and meaning as a way forward.

If the woman refuses to be 'inherited' by any of his relatives (brother or nephew) she risks being chased away from the marital home leaving her children.

Abuse [of lobola] has crept in through commercialization of the transaction and through greed.

3 The dynamics of lobola, the marriage institution and gender rights within families

Customary marriages which are normally validated by the payment of lobola like other marriages such as civil and religious marriages are embedded in an androcratic social model which reinforces the inequality in gender relations, hence impeding women's control over their sexuality and reproductive rights.

As mentioned in the previous sections, all marriages have implications for women's rights. Customary marriages which are normally validated by the payment of *lobola* like other marriages such as civil and religious marriages are embedded in an androcratic social model which reinforces the inequality in gender relations, hence impeding women's control over their sexuality and reproductive rights. This puts their physical and mental health at risk. In this section we will discuss the linkage and implications of *lobola* for women's rights.

What are women's reproductive rights?

Borrowing from the advances of feminist debates, women's reproductive rights can be understood as the rights of a woman to control her own sexuality and reproductive capacity: making decisions on the number of children she has; their spacing and timing and also whether to have them or not. Regarding this Sonia Correa and Rosalind Petchesky (1995) wrote:

> ...the terrain of reproductive and sexual rights can be defined in terms of power and resources: power to make informed decisions about one's own fertility and sexual activity and resources to carry out such decisions safely and effectively.

The argument of these authors is associated with the basic human rights principles of bodily integrity, personhood, equality and diversity.

The concept of reproductive rights as well as the demand for them represents a recent victory for the feminist movement, firstly in the political field and at the theoretical level. After the Universal Declaration of Human Rights (1948), human rights for a long time were understood in such a way as to exclude women as equals. Despite the adoption in 1966 by the General Assembly of two pacts: the international civil and political rights pact and the international social and cultural rights pact, there was no improvement in gender relations. Women's rights were still neglected although women's social rights in the context of second-generation human rights had begun to be considered. The inclusion of women's rights was done in such a way that they remained invisible subjects without their own person-

ality. Because of such shortcomings, the equality prescribed in international instruments has limited significance for women in the real world. For example, discriminatory practices that hold women in a subservient position and lead to their exclusion from public life have generally not been seen as a violation of human rights and fundamental freedoms of women (Reed Boland *et al.* 1995).

Various international instruments have been emerging slowly in an attempt to incorporate women's rights into international instruments and policies and projects of the United Nations. Among these, the Convention on the Elimination of All Forms of Discrimination Against Women (CEDAW) is outstanding because it specifically addresses the issue of discrimination against women. In this convention women's rights were explicit. There are specific provisions which address the issue of women's reproductive rights found in the following sections: Articles 5*b*, 10*f*, 11*f*, 10*f* (2*a*), 11*f*, 2*d*, 12 and 16*e*.

...discriminatory practices that hold women in a subservient position and lead to their exclusion from public life have generally not been seen as a violation of human rights and fundamental freedoms of women

Article 5*b*
This article ensures that family education includes a proper understanding of maternity as a social function and recognises the common responsibility of men and women in the upbringing and development of their children, it being understood that the interests of the children are the primary considerations in all cases;

Article 10*f*
This article deals with access to specific educational information and to help to ensure the health and wellbeing of families, including information and advice on family planning;

Article 11*f*
This article covers the right to health protection and safe working conditions, including safeguarding the function of reproduction;

Article 10*f (2 a)*
This prohibits, subject to the imposition of sanctions, dismissal on the grounds of pregnancy or maternity leave and discrimination in dismissals on the basis of marital status;

Article 11*f* (*2d*)
This provides special protection to women during pregnancy from types of work proved to be harmful to them;

Article 12
This states parties shall take all appropriate measures to eliminate discrimination against women in the field of health care to ensure access to health care services, including those related to family planning, on a basis of equality of men and women; and
Notwithstanding the provisions of paragraph one of this article, it states parties shall ensure women have appropriate services in connection with pregnancy, confinement and post-natal period, granting free services where necessary as well as adequate nutrition during pregnancy and lactation;

Article 16*e*
This grants the same right to women to decide freely and responsibly on the number and spacing of their children, and to have access to the information, education and means to enable them to exercise these rights.

In the Cairo Conference on Population and Development (ICPD) in 1994 women's human rights were debated and after much resistance, their reproductive and sexual rights were explicitly recognized. This conference and the Beijing Platform for Action were the most important in the area of women's sexual and reproductive rights because they defined the two terms explicitly:

> Reproductive rights embrace certain human rights that are already recognized in national laws, international laws and international human rights documents and other consensus documents. These rights rest on the recognition of the basic right of all couples and individuals to decide freely and responsibly the number, spacing and timing of their children and to have the information and means to do so, and the right to attain the highest standard of

sexual and reproductive health. It also includes their rights to make decisions concerning reproduction free of discrimination, coercion and violence, as expressed in human rights documents.

Women's reproductive rights under international human rights law are therefore a composite of a number of separate human rights, as follows:

- The right to health, reproductive health and family planning
- The right to decide the number and spacing of children
- The right to marry and found a family
- The right to life, liberty and security
- The right to be free from gender discrimination
- The right to be free from sexual assault and exploitation
- The right not to be subjected to torture or other cruel, inhuman, or degrading treatment or punishment
- The right to modify customs that discriminate against women
- The right to privacy
- The right to enjoy scientific progress and to consent to experimentation

Most WLSA countries have already ratified the international instruments mentioned which have the potential to protect women's rights. The declaration by heads of state or government of the Southern African Development Community (SADC) on the Prevention and Eradication of Violence Against Women and Children is another important milestone in our region. We, as part of the women's movement, and women's rights activists have to demand that our governments honour the commitments made by SADC heads of state.

The declaration by heads of state or government of the Southern African Development Community (SADC) on the Prevention and Eradication of Violence Against Women and Children is another important milestone in our region.

Despite all these advances resulting from women's movements demanding rights, the exercise of reproductive rights by women is still a long way from reality. This is because of the patriarchal model which dominates our societies on the one hand and traditions and negative practices which are still in place in our societies on the other. There is prevalence in our countries of gross violations of women's rights deriving from what we have already mentioned. The practices of *lobola* give more power to men than women in marriage so reaffirm and reinforce the violations of women's rights, as we will analyze in the next section.

Constitutions and provisions on discrimination in reproductive rights should be challenged where they exist to ensure that there is a non-discriminatory provision. In most of these countries the provision states that there shall be no discrimination on the basis of sex, gender or race, but under the same constitution (Zambia, Zimbabwe, Lesotho) allows discrimination on the basis of personal laws and custom. Swaziland does not have a constitution presently, but is in the process of drafting one and some of these ideas should be enshrined in the new constitution.

Implications of *lobola* for women's rights

As Sonia Correa and Rosalind Petchesky (1995) argued, the basic human rights that are associated with personhood, bodily integrity, equality and diversity are very important for women. Taking into account the principle of personhood which means to consider women as principal actors and decision-makers in matters of reproduction and sexuality — as subjects not merely objects (Correa *et al.*, 1995), the significance of *lobola* sometimes compromises the principle of personhood. Women's rights are fundamentally about the struggle to make women's voices heard and heeded. This implies that women must have the upper hand in expressing their views on health policies and programmes. This situation is examined in two dimensions: the first is the family and the other deals with the state's intervention on population policy issues.

Women's rights are fundamentally about the struggle to make women's voices heard and heeded.

At family level, in most of the WLSA countries, women do not take decisions in matters relating to their reproductive and sexual rights. When *lobola* has been transferred in most of these countries decisions relating to reproductive and sexual rights are transferred to the husband and his family. In Zambia among the Ngoni, marriage involves the permanent transfer of a woman's fertility to a man's group that is validated by the transfer of cattle and made permanent by the birth of children. This is indicated by expressly referring to the transfer of cattle in specific terms. Among the Basotho such cattle are called *ngoana ke oa khomo* which translates to 'cattle beget children'. This is a common saying among the Bantu and it basically means that when cattle are transferred in marriage it is for the children. In Lesotho, among the cattle that are transferred to the woman's family one of them is referred to as *khomo ea seboko* which

means a cow that transfers the procreative function of the girl to the family or clan of her husband.

The significance of *lobola* is obvious in some of these countries in cases where *lobola* has not been paid because the children do not belong to the father and his lineage but belong to the maternal family or lineage. Among the Tswana of Botswana, the Shona of Zimbabwe, the Tumbuka of Malawi and the Swazi of Swaziland, children born out of wedlock are the responsibility of the maternal grandfather. In Botswana these are referred to as *go epa ngwana* or *go tsala ngwana*, in Zimbabwe, *vana vasina baba* and in Swaziland they are known as *bantfwana betintfombi*.[5] In the three countries where *lobola* has not been paid the father of the child is denied any entitlement to *lobola* paid for his first daughter. In Botswana he is not allowed to participate in the negotiations which is the domain of the daughter's maternal grandparents, uncles and aunts unless he pays immediately for the girl's mother in a case where they are still together. In Swaziland and Malawi, the father is allowed to 'buy' the child if he has not paid *lobola*. He pays two beasts for a girl-child and one for a boy-child and this gives him the rights of guardianship. In Zimbabwe, *lobola* for the daughter may be claimed as *lobola* for the mother as WLSA Zimbabwe learned recently during the Magaya documentation where the *lobola* for her daughter, Talkmore, was given to Venia's father because Talkmore's father had not paid *lobola* for Venia (WLSA, 2001).

The transfer of the woman's fertility or reproductive rights effectively means that the man and his group will have full rights over her reproductive capabilities and they will take decisions on the number of children and whether there will be children at all. In all the WLSA countries among the patrilineal societies, women cannot take decisions relating to the number of children they have, when and whether to have them at all. In Botswana, for example, women for whom *bogadi* has been paid — whether married under customary or general law — have no say in the number of children that they want. In most of these countries women cannot use contraceptives freely unless they get permission from their husbands. This also includes cases where a woman's life is at risk, for example, if she has needs to stop reproducing due to health problems. Usually those who

> *In all the WLSA countries among the patrilineal societies, women cannot take decisions relating to the number of children they have, when and whether to have them at all.*

---

[5] All these terms mean *fatherless children* and are used in a derogatory manner.

control her fertility will not give permission to stop and the result for most women is to continue bearing children until they die.

In fact in our patriarchal societies the attitude is that the woman has to continue bearing the children as long as she can. In one case in Mozambique, for example, when a man was asked why he does not use contraceptives or allow his wives to use contraceptives, he said that it was necessary for a woman to bring out all the children in her belly until God decided it was enough. This is the attitude in most of our societies, particularly in those where *lobola* is paid. In Zimbabwe the number of cattle is proportionate to the number of children that a wife is expected to bear, particularly among the Ndebele. In Malawi, Swaziland, Mozambique and Lesotho, a wife is pressurised to produce a large number of children, particularly male children. Because of the patriarchal nature of these societies, girl children are not considered important whereas male children are considered important for the continuation of the lineage. Girl children are marriage bound and their only value is to bring *lobola* to their families. All the above clearly speaks to the fact that:

> …children are born for men, and even the language speaks to this patriarchal fact, even in matrilineal lineage systems, because the men of the lineage are the final decision makers (McFadden, 1994: 64).

In all these countries childless marriages are not tolerated where *lobola* has been paid, there is no divorce and death is not the end of the marriage. In most of these countries childlessness, divorce or death results in the return of *lobola* or a substitute is found to replace the wife. In the case of barrenness her unproductive womb has to be replaced by a productive one. The wife is usually not consulted or her views considered when this is done and this is a violation of her personhood. In Zambia, Mozambique, Zimbabwe and Swaziland a brother's daughter or younger sister is brought in to replace her womb and in Swaziland this is known as *inhlanti* whilst in Mozambique it is called *hlampsa*. The woman in most of these cases has no say as McFadden (1994) argues:

> All these practices are the most extreme expressions of the absence of a concept of respect for the personhood of the female in our societies. These

Girl children … are marriage bound and their only value is to bring lobola to their families.

practices, buttressed by other related practices like arranged marriages and the use of mainly female children to compensate a death in another family speak loudly to the absence of the recognition that an African woman is a person in her self, of herself, as a human being, as a citizen of a country, and that her right of personhood is as sacred as any other woman's right.

In some situations the state contributes to the woman's loss of personhood through certain policies. For example, in most of our countries the state usually takes decisions about fertility control for population control purposes. In WLSA countries the states normally encourage the use of contraceptives for population control rather than empowering women to take decisions as subjects. So women are used as objects and this violates their personhood. In most instances women are not consulted on types of contraception, they have to make do with what is available on the market and there is no post-evaluation on the effects and their perception of the product. In Zimbabwe, for example, Depo Provera was discontinued by the state yet there is evidence that it is one of the most preferred forms of contraception for women. In most instances women are not even educated on the advantages and disadvantages of what is available.

In WLSA countries the states normally encourage the use of contraceptives for population control rather than empowering women to take decisions as subjects.

Bodily integrity

The concept of bodily integrity means the right to security in and control over your body. It is very closely related to or sometimes taken as the same as personhood. As Correa *et al.* (1995) pointed out, this lies at the core of reproductive and sexual freedom, as they state:

> ...in its specific applications, the bodily integrity reminds us that while reproductive and sexual rights are necessarily social, they are also irreducibly personal.

They share this conception with Fredman and Isaacs (1993) and Petchesky (1990). Taking into consideration what has already been mentioned, women's bodily integrity is systematically violated by diverse forms where *lobola* has been paid and also in

civil marriages, where it has not been paid, by other provisions such as the marital power which is vested in the husband. In most of the WLSA countries women's bodily integrity is violated and examples of violations are found in the following:

- No right to use family planning
- Women treated as property
- Violence against women

When a woman wants to practise family planning she has to seek permission from her husband.

As has already been pointed out, women may not use contraceptives without the consent of their husbands. When a woman wants to practise family planning she has to seek permission from her husband. In Swaziland, for example, clinics used to require the husband's consent before they could give contraceptives to a woman. In cases where a woman uses contraceptives without permission, she keeps it secret but if the husband finds out she may be in trouble. Also, for other medical needs such as an operation, the husband needs to sign to give his consent. This is problematic and risky for women in cases of emergency where having to locate the husband for his consent may jeopardize her life. The same situation exists in Lesotho, Zimbabwe and Botswana where the wife cannot use contraceptives if the husband does not consent. In Zimbabwe it has been reported that one woman was even murdered by her husband when he discovered that she was taking oral contraceptives. At times even when her health is put at risk by having children, a woman will continue to bear them which means that not only has she lost control over her reproduction but she has also lost control over her body and her health. Situations have arisen where doctors advised women not to have any more children — for instance because of high blood pressure and other health-related problems — and yet they ignore this warning because their husbands did not consent and this has resulted in their death. This is clearly a violation of their bodily integrity.

Women as property

Lobola negotiations resemble a market where there is buying and selling of women because a price for the woman is usually negotiated. This is manifested in many ways in our societies. In Swaziland for example, a working woman may be expected to hand over her pay cheque to her husband who bought her productive power. Husbands usually claim that they are the ones

who give permission to their wives to be in employment because they believe that they own them and hence demand the fruits of their labour. It is also common in Swaziland to find that married urban women take leave from work during the ploughing and weeding season and go to their rural marital home to perform these duties. In Lesotho and Swaziland, a girl from the royal family has a higher *lobola* charged for her than a commoner.

Violence against women

In most of the WLSA countries violence against women (physical, sexual and psychological) is common and there are indications that some of this violence is directly linked to *lobola*. In Mozambique, for example, women who are victims of violence at the hands of their husbands seldom present their problem to their families because they will not listen to them since they have already spent the *lobola*. In most of these countries the woman is pressurised to endure the violence because if she leaves, the *lobola* may be demanded back, or part of it demanded back if she has had children in the marriage. Most women have been found to bear the violence against them, some of which is sexual violence.

Marital rape is not a crime in most of the WLSA countries and that demonstrates the vulnerability of women in marriage. The Non-consensual Sex in Marriage (NCSM, 2000) organization reported that in most parts of the world a woman is considered to have agreed on her wedding day to sexual relations for the rest of her life: her consent or not to sex in married life becomes irrelevant, subjugated to her husband's wishes and actions. Whether this is achieved by coercion or force, her right to control her own body is denied and a husband's ability to abuse her sexually is unhindered. Women and girls are raped and sexually assaulted in untold numbers every day: their abusers have the protection of the marriage which legitimizes some of these violations, for instance the non-criminalization of marital rape. Some countries actually reward rape with marriage, allowing the rapist to escape prosecution by offering to marry his 'victim' (NCSM, June 2000: 1). Most of the WLSA countries' offices have attended to clients who have been beaten by their husbands because they have paid *lobola* for them. In Botswana, for example, where *lobola* has been paid and the

Marital rape is not a crime in most of the WLSA countries and that demonstrates the vulnerability of women in marriage.

woman is not 'performing sexually according to standard' or does not appear to be meeting expectations, she is subjected to sexual and physical violence which can be attributed to the fact that the man is probably not getting his money's worth. In Zimbabwe a woman may suffer psychological abuse by being denounced publicly for failing to meet a man's standard of sexual performance as alleged by Mr Mandizvidza of Chitungwiza as to the reason he was applying for a divorce from his wife. In addition to claiming that the wife had all of a sudden become 'incompetent in bed' the woman had had her career opportunities compromised as the husband had refused her the opportunity to seek formal employment by insisting that she be a full-time housewife (*The Herald*, Thursday June 21, 2001). Some women have suffered rape and severe beatings at the hands of their husbands when they have suggested the use of condoms and such men justify their actions saying *ke duetse bogadi jo bo tletseng*, meaning 'I paid *lobola* in full and no cow was deducted to compensate for the use of condoms'.

Some women have suffered rape and severe beatings at the hands of their husbands when they have suggested the use of condoms

All the above speaks to the absence of women's bodily integrity. Women's reproductive rights are human rights and it is important that women themselves should have some control which should include:

- The right to decide how many children to have, and when or whether to have them;
- The right to have information and means to control one's fertility; and
- The right to control one's body.

Since these are violated in one way or the other in WLSA countries, women's fundamental human rights are violated too. This is clearly demonstrated by women's lack of capacity to seek family-planning facilities, including abortion, in cases of unwanted pregnancies. If women could access these without fear they would be able to claim back their bodies and take decisions on the number of children, whether to have them and when to have them. If this happened in our countries it would be a victory for the women's movement and women in general. This is a challenge to all women in the world and the Africa region and southern Africa in particular where WLSA countries are geographically located.

The fact that a woman does not have control over her fertility has a negative impact on her health. This situation is not just one where the husband owns and controls her reproductive capacity but it also gives him the right to decide whether she lives or dies. For example, the husband has to decide whether she is operated on or not and in a case where she has to stop reproducing because her health is in danger, the husband may refuse and she could die in childbirth. Clearly this is an area where policy and legal intervention is necessary in order to protect women's lives.

The fight against *lobola* should increase women's access to their rights both in private and public life. Rights in this case include women's sexual and reproductive rights, and also the right to nutrition, education and health. This is the great battle for feminists because without women's access to these resources — be they material or cultural — the social relations between genders, such as relations of power, will never change. All these are important to preserve women's personhood and bodily integrity.

The fight against lobola should increase women's access to their rights both in private and public life. Rights... include women's sexual and reproductive rights, and also the right to nutrition, education and health.

4 Conclusion, recommendations and possible areas of action

The significance of *lobola* as a women's rights issue derives from women often being excluded from the process of negotiations and exchange. Most importantly, the bride is not always consulted on whether she consents to the process of *lobola*. This lack of consultation and choice has adverse implications for perceiving women as commodities. The process of *lobola* negotiations and renegotiations can be equated with bargaining. The sense of value placed on women in this process of negotiation can equate them with commodities on the market.

The process of lobola negotiations and renegotiations can be equated with bargaining.

The arguments advanced show that *lobola* can impoverish the family. While it can be said that *lobola* is the responsibility of the man's family, this is not always the case. For instance, if a man is marrying a second or subsequent wife, he becomes exclusively responsible for *lobola* payment. Resources from the nuclear family may be diverted and used to acquire a second wife (WLSA Zimbabwe, 1997a & b). A similar scenario is noted in poor families where parents are unable to contribute towards payment of *lobola* for their sons. In this case, if the man is employed, he becomes responsible for providing for his family and would therefore ultimately pay for his own *lobola*. This has significant implications for the relationship of these men and the influence they have on their families.

The analysis has shown that *lobola* as currently practised in the seven WLSA countries is a commoditisation of women by men. This is because the negotiations are almost always between the male members of the two families while women are kept in the background. These negotiations, like any commercial transactions, are long, drawn-out processes of bargaining.

The payment of lobola implies that the husband's family has a right to the woman's reproductive capacity as well as the remains of her body after death.

The common anthropological explanations put forward for the existence of a custom such as *lobola* are that it validates or legalizes a marriage and transfers rights in children of the partners. Others argue that *lobola* is given as a token of appreciation and compensation of some sort to the family of the bride. This can be material, economic, or symbolic. *Lobola* then plays a symbolic role in creating and maintaining relationships across African societies. The payment of *lobola* implies that the husband's family has a right to the woman's reproductive capacity as well as the remains of her body after death. The contemporary view in southern Africa is to slightly modify indigenous ideas and behaviour but not completely abandon traditional values that reflect and symbolize the identity of a particular community.

The practice of *lobola* operates to harm women not as individuals but as a group. This is because customary law only permits men the right to pay *lobola* and therefore continues subordination of women as a group. There is need to balance the constitutional right to equality and cultural practices.

Recommendations

Southern Africa needs to pay considerable attention to the development and future of customary law and rid itself of some of its negative consequences for women. It is recommended that *lobola* should not be a determinant of validity or otherwise of marriage. Marriage systems should be unified into one general law that would apply to everyone. This analysis has shown that family law touches upon deeply entrenched customs and practices that cannot be changed by a stroke of a legislative pen. In spite of what has been said, however, it might be possible to introduce a single, integrated body of law that would make uniform regulations where possible and at the same time allow for dualism where necessary. A unified marriage system in courts should reflect some of the provisions on women's rights during marriage and within a family. Sections that give men marital power should be removed.

Lobola should be abolished in order to take away the 'purchase power' perception tied to the practice that gives men repressive power over women and perpetuates and exacerbates gender violence against women and children. In advocating for its abolition, there is also a need to sensitize the entire nation and region about the practice of *lobola* and its implications for women. The sensitization should include law and policy makers and the men and women in the communities.

Advocacy around issues of marriage could help women with information on different marriage regimes and the implications of choosing one. The advocacy issues should be around marriage and how women can be empowered in this institution and protection of women's reproductive rights. To achieve this, and short of abolishing *lobola*, we can perhaps take a leaf from the Angola Family Law based on the fundamental principle of the legal recognition of equality between women and men in all family matters. The equality is also guaranteed in the Angolan national constitution. Within a marriage, the wife and husband

It is recommended that lobola should not be a determinant of validity or otherwise of marriage. Marriage systems should be unified into one general law that would apply to everyone.

have the same rights and obligations under various situations as stipulated in the law of the country (SARDC, 2000: 145)

The seven WLSA countries need to adopt effective means or measures to promote and fulfill the reproductive rights of women and men, and address practices that perpetuate gender inequalities such as *lobola* that are directly relevant to decisions about sexual and reproductive rights.

Areas of action

The practices of the people contribute a great deal to what law is and what changes can work. Many women's lives are influenced more by living law than by state law.

In deciding on the appropriate action to change things for the better, regard must always be taken of the fact that law is more than what happens in parliament and state courts. The practices of the people contribute a great deal to what law is and what changes can work. Many women's lives are influenced more by living law than by state law. This means taking a more holistic approach that aims not only at changing state laws but also at influencing the living law that is the area where the majority of women will be found. Since the family has been noted by WLSA studies[6] to be playing a vital role in women's lives, it is important that the changes should not leave them isolated, vulnerable, and even poorer because they do not have the family to support them. It becomes important to target the power structures in the family that leave women at the bottom of the hierarchy. The family has to be more egalitarian and protect all its members especially those who are vulnerable like women, the aged and children by removing practices that perpetuate this inequality. If these factors change then women would be in a position to decide when and how many children to have without fear of being held in contempt by the family or by society.

This approach will have as one of its key elements the empowerment of women that requires:

---

[6] *Botswana families and women's rights in a changing environment*, Botswana, 1997.
Family belonging in Lesotho, Lesotho, 1998.
Family in transition — the experience of Swaziland, WLSA Swaziland, 1998.
Changing family in Zambia, Zambia, 1997.
Family in a changing environment in Mozambique, WLSA Mozambique, 1997.
Continuity and change: The family in Zimbabwe, WLSA Zimbabwe, 1997.
Paradigms of exclusion: Women's access to resources in Zimbabwe, WLSA Zimbabwe, 1997.

> ...the radical transformation of all social structures
> and laws that perpetuate women's subordination, in
> order to end male domination (Dyring, 1994 p 34).

This applies to the redistribution of and control over material assets and intellectual resources as well as ideology. *Lobola* is one of the practices that underpins the ideologies regarding the inequalities between women and men — and denies women any decision-making power over their lives. Practices such as *lobola* are some of those that, for instance, perpetuate male dominance in sexual relations and decisions on the number and spacing of children. If the woman is the one who bears children, denying her the right to decide whether to have children and how many children to have seriously undermines her reproductive rights. Thus we need to work for improvements that will lead to a change in the social status of women including those who are poor and depend on others.

If the woman is the one who bears children, denying her the right to decide whether to have children at all and on the number of such children seriously undermines her reproductive rights.

The issue of *lobola* is one in which the role of the state is weak yet it would be easy for the state to strengthen women's control over their reproduction by adopting policies and laws to help women achieve this. States can create social, political, economic and legal conditions that permit everyone access to empowering resources.

Women can then advocate for transformative approaches (enabling laws and customs) that seek to change gender roles and create more gender-equitable relationships, for example, debates that question the validity and relevance of cultural practices such as *lobola*.

Effective legislation should be introduced and implemented against gender-based violence. Social and judicial action is needed to combat gender–based violence, including sexual abuse and domestic violence. WLSA studies have demonstrated how socio-cultural practices such as *lobola* reinforce the subordinate status of women within the family and in marriage.

Bibliography

Andrade, X. *et al.*
    Families in a changing environment in Mozambique, WLSA
    Mozambique, University Press, Maputo, 1997.
    Women and inheritance in Mozambique, WLSA Mozambique,
    University Press, Maputo, 1994.

Aphane *et al.*, *Family in transition: the experience of Swaziland*, WLSA
    Swaziland, Ruswanda Publishing Bureau, Swaziland, 1998.

Arnfred Signe, 'Reflections on family, trends of change, *lobola* and
    polygyny', in *Changing families, changing laws*, Women and Law
    in Southern Africa Working Paper No. 9. WLSA, Harare,

Arthur Maria Jose, *Politicas da desiqualdade?* Primeiros elemntos para
    uma avaliacao das politicas eprogramas de genero Governo e das
    ONGs apos.

Beijing 1995-1999; Forum Mulher, Maputo, Mozambique, 2000.

Chigwedere, A., *Lobola, the pros and cons*, Books for Africa, Harare,
    1982.

Colson, Elisabeth, *Marriage and the family among the plateau Tonga of
    Northern Rhodesia*, Manchester University Press, Manchester, 1958.

Corea Sonia *et al.*, 'Reproductive and sexual rights — a feminist
perspective', in *Population policies reconsidered: Health,
empowerment and rights*, 1994.

Department of Women's Affairs, *Report on a review of all laws
    affectingthe status of women in Botswana*, Gaborone, 1998.

Dow, U. and P. Kidd, *Women, marriage and inheritance*, WLSA
    Botswana, Gaborone, 1994.

Dyring, A., *Forgotten fact: population policy reconsidered*, SAREC,
    Stockholm, 1994.

Emecheta, Buchi, 'From the discussion', in Ngcobo Lauretta's *African
    motherhood — myth and reality*, 2000.

Henri, Junod, Usos e Costumes dos Bantos, Vida Social, 2a Edicao,
    1974.

Kidd, P. *et al.*, *Botswana families and women's rights in a changing
    environment*, WLSA, 1997.

Letuka, P. *et al.*, *Family belonging for women in Lesotho*, WLSA, Marija,
    Lesotho, 1998.

MacFadden, P. 'Gender, power and patriarchy' in WLSA Working Paper
    No. 9, *Changing families, changing laws*, 1994.

Maqutu, W.C.M., *Contemporary family law in Lesotho*, National
    University Press, Maseru, 1992.

Mati, J.K.G. *et al.*, *Reproductive health in Africa*, John Hopkins
    Programme for International Education in Gynaecology and
    Obstetrics, Maryland, 1984.

May, J., *Changing people, changing laws*, Mambo Press, Gweru, 1987.

Mokobi, K. and P. Kidd, 'Marriage and inheritance: the chameleon changes its colours' in *Widowhood, inheritance laws, customs and practices in southern Africa*, W. Ncube and J. Stewart (eds), WLSA, Harare, 1995.

Myburg, A.C., Papers on indigenous laws in southern Africa, J.L.van Schaik (Pvt) Ltd, Pretoria, 1990.

Nafis, Sadik, 'Situacao da populacao mundial' in *Direito de Escolher: direitos reprodutivos e saude reproductiva*, 1997.

Ncube, W. *et al., Paradigms of exclusion: Women's access to resources in Zimbabwe*, WLSA Zimbabwe, Harare, 1997.

NCSM paper on Non-consensual Sex in Marriage, June 2000.

Nhapo, T., *Marriage and divorce in Swazi law and custom*, Websters (Pty) Ltd. Mbabane , 1992.

Ngulbe, Naboth, *Some aspects of growing up in Zambia*, Nalinga Consultancy, Sol-Consult A/S Limited, Lusaka, 1989.

Osorio, Conceicao, Violencia Contra a Jovem e construcao da identidade feminina, Maputo, 1997.

Richards, Audrey, *Bemba marriage and present economic conditions*, Rhodes Livingstone Paper No. 4, Manchester University Press, Manchester, 1940.

SARDC, *Beyond inequalities – women in southern Africa*, Harare, 2000.

Schapera, I., 'Kinship and politics' in *Tswana History*, Journal of the Royal Anthropological Institute, Vol. 93 (2), 1963.
Handbook of Tswana law and custom.

Frank Cass, *Native land tenure in the 1943 Bechuanaland Protectorate*, Lavedale Press, Alice, 1938.

Stewart, J. and A. Armstrong, *The legal situation of women in southern Africa*, University of Zimbabwe Publications, Harare, 1990.

Stolke, Veronica, 'Direito Reprodutivos' in Direitos Reprodutivos Sandra Azeredo Verena Stolke cord, 1991.

Toubia, Nahid, 'Women's reproductive and sexual rights' in *Gender violence and women's rights in Africa*, Centre for Women's Global Leadership, New Jersey, 1994.

Touwen, Anne, *Gender and development in Zambia — empowerment of women through local non-governmental organizations*, Eburon Publishers, Delft, 1996.

Weinrich, A.K.H., *African marriage in Zimbabwe and the impact of Christianity*, Mambo Press, Harare, 1982.

WLSA,
Pregnancy and childbirth – Joy or Despair? Gender-generated reproductive crimes of violence, WLSA-Zimbabwe, Harare, 2001.
Venia Magaya's sacrifice: A case of custom gone awry, WLSA- Zimbabwe, Harare, 2001.
Inheritance in Zambia: laws and practices, WLSA-Zambia, Lusaka, 1994.

www.ingramcontent.com/pod-product-compliance
Lightning Source LLC
Chambersburg PA
CBHW080926050426
42334CB00055B/2829